Readers' Theater: How to Put on a Production

Fettuccine and Four-Leaf Clovers

A Readers' Theater Script and Guide

Looking Glass Library

An Imprint of Magic Wagon
abdopublishing.com

By Nancy K. Wallace   Illustrated by Nina Mata

To my brother Rob, who can answer any question about the weather. —NKW
To my parents, my loving husband Aaron & my darling Aria. —NM

abdopublishing.com

Published by Magic Wagon, a division of ABDO, PO Box 398166, Minneapolis, Minnesota 55439.
Copyright © 2016 by Abdo Consulting Group, Inc. International copyrights reserved in all countries. No part of this book may be reproduced in any form without written permission from the publisher. Looking Glass Library™ is a trademark and logo of Magic Wagon.

Printed in the United States of America, North Mankato, Minnesota.
042015
092015

THIS BOOK CONTAINS
RECYCLED MATERIALS

Written by Nancy K. Wallace
Illustrations by Nina Mata
Edited by Heidi M.D. Elston, Megan M. Gunderson & Bridget O'Brien
Designed by Laura Mitchell

Library of Congress Cataloging-in-Publication Data

Wallace, Nancy K.
   Fettuccine and four-leaf clovers : a readers' theater script and guide / by Nancy K. Wallace ; illustrated by Nina Mata.
      pages cm. -- (Readers' theater: how to put on a production set 2)
   ISBN 978-1-62402-112-1
 1. Saint Patrick's Day--Juvenile literature. 2. Theater--Production and direction--Juvenile literature. 3. Readers' theater--Juvenile literature. I. Mata, Nina, 1981- illustrator. II. Title.
   PS3623.A4436F48 2015
   812'.6--dc23
                                      2015000186

Table of Contents

Celebrate with a Play!

Everyone loves holidays! Some schools and libraries hold programs or assemblies to commemorate special occasions. This series offers fun plays to help celebrate six different holidays at your school or library. You can even sell tickets and use your play as a fund-raiser.

Readers' theater can be done very simply. The performers sit on stools or chairs onstage. They don't have to memorize their lines. They just read them.

Adapted readers' theater looks more like a regular play. The stage includes scenery and props. The performers wear makeup and costumes. They move around to show the action. But, they still carry their scripts.

Readers' theater scripts can also be used for puppet shows. The performers stand behind a curtain, move the puppets, and read their scripts.

Find a place large enough to put on a play. An auditorium with a stage is ideal. A classroom will work, too. Choose a date and ask permission to use the space. Advertise your play with posters and flyers. Place them around your school and community. Tell your friends and family. Everyone enjoys watching a fun performance!

Tickets and Playbills

Tickets and playbills can be handwritten or designed on a computer. Be sure tickets include the title of the play. They should list the date, time, and location of the performance.

A playbill is a printed program. The front of a playbill has the title of the play, the date, and the time. The cast and crew are listed inside. Be sure to have enough playbills for the audience and cast. Pass them out at the door as the audience enters.

The Crew

Next, a crew is needed. The show can't go on without these important people! Some jobs can be combined for a small show.

Director — organizes everyone and everything in the show.

Costume Designer — designs and borrows or makes all the costumes.

Stage Manager — makes sure everything runs smoothly.

Lighting Designer — runs spotlights and other lighting.

Set Designer — plans and makes scenery.

Prop Manager — finds, makes, and keeps track of props.

Special Effects Crew — takes care of sound and other special effects.

Sets

At a readers' theater production, the performers can sit on stools at the front of the room. An adapted readers' theater production or full play will require sets and props. A set is the background that creates the setting for each scene. A prop is an item the actors use onstage.

Scene 1 takes place in the hallway of the school. Paint some pieces of cardboard to look like lockers.

Scene 2 and **scene 4** take place in Mr. O'Brien's classroom. Set the scene with desks and chairs. Include a whiteboard on wheels or an easel with a tablet or piece of poster board on it.

Scene 3 is at Nicholas's house. Use a large table, a small table, and three chairs. Place the chairs so that the side of the large table toward the audience is open. Place the small table off to one side.

Scene 5 takes place in the cafeteria. Use card tables to hold the cookies, flags, photos, and music player.

Props

- 2 backpacks
- Whiteboard or tablet on easel
- Marker
- Bottles of water

- Single plate of cookies
- Flags from various countries
- Plates of cookies from various countries

- Music player
- Newspaper clippings
- Magazine clippings
- Photographs

The Cast

Decide who will play each part. Each person in the cast will need a script. All of the performers should practice their lines. Reading lines aloud over and over will help the performers learn them. *Fettuccine and Four-Leaf Clovers* needs the following cast:

Cody — a student in Mr. O'Brien's class

Nicholas — Cody's best friend

Ana — a student in Mr. O'Brien's class

Olivia — a student in Mr. O'Brien's class

Mr. O'Brien — Cody's teacher

Class — the students in Mr. O'Brien's class

Parents and Students — people who come to the final event

Makeup and Costumes

Makeup artists have a big job! Every cast member wears makeup. And, stage makeup needs to be brighter and heavier than regular makeup. Buy several basic shades of mascara, foundation, blush, and lipstick. Apply with a new cotton ball or swab for each cast member to avoid spreading germs.

Costume designers set the scene just as much as set designers. They borrow costumes or adapt old clothing for each character. Ask adults for help finding and sewing costumes.

Most of the performers in this play can wear regular clothes they would wear to school. There are a few exceptions.

Cody and **Nicholas** should wear backpacks in scene 1. Cody should wear a watch.

Mr. O'Brien should wear a shirt and tie.

Parents in scene 5 should dress like adults.

Rehearsals and Stage Directions

After you decide to put on a play, it is important to set up a rehearsal schedule. Choose a time everyone can attend, such as after school or on weekends. Try to have at least five rehearsals before the performance.

Everyone should practice together as a team, even though individual actors will be reading their own scripts. This will help the play sound like a conversation, instead of separate lines. Onstage, actors should act like their characters even when they aren't speaking.

In the script, stage directions are in parentheses. They are given from the performer's point of view, not the audience's. Actors face the audience when performing, so left is on their left and right is on their right.

Some theater terms may be unfamiliar:

Curtains — the main curtain at the front of the stage.

House — the area in which the audience sits.

Wings — the part of the stage on either side that the audience can't see.

Script: Fettuccine and Four-Leaf Clovers
Scene 1: The Hallway of North Side School

(Use painted lockers as a backdrop. Decorate with green crepe paper and shamrocks. Cody and Nicholas enter stage left wearing backpacks.)

Cody: I'm really sick of green! Next, they'll be serving green mashed potatoes at lunch.

Nicholas: Yuck!

Cody: Or green meatloaf! *(Cody makes a face.)*

Nicholas: Gross! Green isn't my favorite color either, but St. Patrick's Day is next Saturday. The whole town is decorated in green!

Cody: Well, I'm not decorating. I'm not even Irish.

Nicholas: Me either, but lots of people are. The parade is a big deal in Brownsville.

Cody: Maybe they should call it Greensville instead.

(The boys laugh.)

Cody: I don't really want to go to the parade. Do you want to come over next Saturday?

Nicholas: Sure. Do you think your grandma would make pizza for lunch? Her pizza is awesome!

Cody: I'll ask. She loves to cook, and it makes her happy when people like what she makes.

Nicholas: Great! I'll be there! Maybe we can ride our bikes down to the park later, too.

Cody: Sounds like a lot more fun than this silly old parade.

Nicholas: Yeah!

(A bell rings.)

Cody: *(Looks at his watch.)* Oh no, we're late for Mr. O'Brien's class!

Nicholas: And your grade is already in trouble!

Cody: *(Shakes his head.)* Too bad Mr. O'Brien doesn't realize I'm a genius.

Nicholas: Better run, genius!

(The boys run off, stage right.)

Scene 2: Mr. O'Brien's Classroom

(Arrange a few desks to look like a classroom. Mr. O'Brien stands sideways, so he doesn't have his back to the audience. He is near a whiteboard on wheels or an easel with a piece of poster board on it. Ana and Olivia sit next to each other. Cody and Nicholas walk in from stage right and sit directly in front of them.)

Mr. O'Brien: I'm glad you could join us, boys! I hope I didn't interrupt your morning chat.

Cody and **Nicholas:** *(Grumbling as they take off their backpacks.)* No, Mr. O'Brien.

Mr. O'Brien: Good, because I have some exciting news!

Cody: *(Whispering.)* I'll bet he wants us to dress in green for the next two weeks.

Mr. O'Brien: Our class is taking on a special project. We'll be running a food booth at next Saturday's St. Patrick's Day parade as a fund-raiser for our class trip.

(Students start whispering back and forth. Cody looks at Nicholas and rolls his eyes.)

Mr. O'Brien: Cody, I'd like you and Nicholas to be in charge.

Cody: *(Waves his hands back and forth in front of himself.)* No, no, no. Mr. O'Brien, Nicholas and I have other plans for that Saturday.

Mr. O'Brien: I think you need to change your plans, boys. This project is worth half your grade for the semester in social studies. And as I remember, a lot of you could use a little help in that department.

(Cody and Nicholas groan.)

Mr. O'Brien: *(Draws numbers on the whiteboard as he is speaking.)* You boys will need to plan committees to buy supplies, ask parents to make or donate food, decorate the booth, and do anything else we'll need for that day to be a huge success.

Cody: Why do we have to do all the work?

Mr. O'Brien: You don't. You'll have the whole class to help you. *(He points at the rest of the class.)* You two are just in charge of dividing up the labor. Each student will be involved in some way. You will be graded both on your individual effort and the success of the whole project. We have less than two weeks to pull this together. Everyone start brainstorming. Tomorrow, we'll divide into the committees Cody and Nicholas come up with.

Cody: Geez! I wasn't even going to go to the stupid parade!

Nicholas: Don't freak out! Ask your mom if you can come over after school. We'll think of something.

Ana: Olivia and I will be glad to help you.

(Olivia nods.)

Cody: I guess we need all the help we can get. Thanks.

Nicholas: We're going to meet at my house after school. Want to come?

Ana and **Olivia:** Sure!

Scene 3: Nicholas's Kitchen

(Place a table in the center of the stage. Ana, Olivia, and Nicholas are sitting down. Cody is pacing. Nicholas has his chair turned backward and is resting his arms on the back. Use another small table as a counter to hold the water bottles and cookies.)

Nicholas: *(Drums his fingers on the table.)* Okay, where do we start?

Cody: *(Handing bottles of water to everyone.)* Mr. O'Brien said we needed some committees. Maybe each of us could head one.

Ana: What committee do you want, Cody? You guys are in charge.

Cody: I don't want to do this at all!

Nicholas: I don't either, but we have to. Do you think Mr. O'Brien picked on us because we were late?

Cody: Probably.

Nicholas: *(Snorts.)* Remind me to never be late again!

Ana: My grandma's Irish. She makes really good Irish potato soup! Do you want me to ask her to cook some for us?

Cody: Yeah, thanks! We're going to need a lot of parents and grandparents to help.

Ana: I can take care of organizing that.

Olivia: My grandma is Polish, but I'm sure she would be glad to bake something.

Nicholas: My family is Hispanic, and my dad's a great cook!

Cody: And we're Italian. Mr. O'Brien should have picked two Irish kids to be in charge! *(Rolls his eyes.)*

Olivia: Too late for that! But I am kind of tired of shamrocks. I was thinking maybe we could decorate the booth with Irish flags. I can print some from the school computers.

Nicholas: That's a good idea. Do you want to be in charge of booth decorations?

Olivia: Okay! I'm sure I can get Grace and Declan to be on my committee.

Cody: *(Puts a plate of cookies down in the middle of the table.)* Hey, let's have cookies at our booth. Everybody loves cookies!

Nicholas: *(Picks up a cookie and starts eating it.)* That's the best idea you've had!

Olivia: I bet everyone in the class would bring cookies.

Ana: My grandma makes awesome Irish shortbread. I could ask her to make some of those, too.

Olivia: My grandpa makes Polish jam sandwich cookies. They are *so* good.

Ana: Oh, I had those once at your house! They're yummy.

Cody: I bet they aren't as good as my mom's Italian anise cookies.

Nicholas: Let's not argue about cookies. All cookies are great!

Cody: Yeah, Nicholas never met a cookie he didn't like.

(Everyone laughs.)

Cody: Let's get back to work. I don't want to fail Mr. O'Brien's class. Olivia, do you need any more ideas for decorations?

Olivia: Maybe we could make a whole string of Irish flags and hang them across the front of the booth.

Cody: It's too bad they're just one kind. It would look better if they were all different flags.

Ana: *(Jumps up from the table.)* Cody, you're a genius!

Cody: *(Smiling and patting himself on the back.)* Well, yeah! Glad you noticed!

Nicholas: *(Gives Cody a soft shove.)* I don't get it. Why is he a genius?

Ana: He just gave me a wonderful idea!

Scene 4: Mr. O'Brien's Classroom

(Props and scenery are the same as for scene 2. Mr. O'Brien stands at stage right. Cody, Nicholas, Ana, and Olivia are seated with other students.)

Mr. O'Brien: Good morning, class! I'm very interested in what Cody and Nicholas have planned for our booth. Are you boys ready to share your ideas?

Cody: Yeah, we're ready! Ana and Olivia offered to help, too. Each of us is in charge of a different committee.

Mr. O'Brien: Good. It sounds like you're very organized. Do you want to come up here and tell the class about it?

Cody: *(Stands up.)* Sure! *(He gestures to Nicholas, Ana, and Olivia.)* Come on! You're part of this, too.

(The four kids move to stage right and stand sideways, facing Mr. O'Brien.)

Ana: I'm in charge of finding parents and grandparents to help cook for the booth.

Olivia: I'm in charge of decorations.

Nicholas: My committee will take care of buying paper products and additional food.

Mr. O'Brien: The school has an account at Stop 'n' Shop. If you make a list of what you need, I'll go with you so we can charge it to the school.

Nicholas: Thanks, Mr. O'Brien!

Mr. O'Brien: And what is your committee doing, Cody?

Cody: We're doing advertising. We'll need to call the local newspaper and radio station. The school TV station will advertise for free. Can we make flyers for everyone to pass out?

Mr. O'Brien: I'm sure we can get permission to do that. I'm really impressed! You've made a great start on this project. Now, why don't you pick people for your committees? Be sure to include everyone.

Ana: Mr. O'Brien? We came up with another idea last night for this project. Can we tell you about it?

Mr. O'Brien: I'd love to hear it!

Ana: Well, my grandma is Irish, but most of the kids in our class aren't. We decided to decorate the booth with flags. Cody said they would look really nice if they were from all different countries. What if we used an around the world theme and had more than one table?

Olivia: We could have pierogi from Poland, fettuccine from Italy, and fajitas from Latin America.

Mr. O'Brien: What about Irish food? This is for St. Patrick's Day!

Ana: My grandma offered to make Irish potato soup and Irish soda bread.

Mr. O'Brien: *(Shakes his head.)* I don't know. I had thought we would have something simple like green lemonade and cookies with green icing. What you're suggesting would be a really big project. How would we cook all of those things?

Cody: What about using the school cafeteria? The parade starts and ends at the school. Everyone could come back here to eat after the parade.

Mr. O'Brien: That might work. I'll see if we can get permission, and help, to use it. Then we'd have room for everyone, places to plug in slow cookers, and space for more booths or tables.

Nicholas: Maybe the kitchen staff would help!

Mr. O'Brien: I think they might! Let me talk to the principal first and see what he says. I'll let you know this afternoon. Maybe this could be our first annual Nationality Day.

Ana: And we thought of it!

Cody: I'm the genius! Don't forget!

Scene 5: The Cafeteria on St. Patrick's Day

(Each small table should be decorated with a paper flag from a specific country. Cover the surface with family pictures cut out of newspapers or magazines. People are walking around, eating and talking. Music plays softly in the background. Mr. O'Brien stands talking with Nicholas and Olivia.)

Mr. O'Brien: You kids did an awesome job! The tables with family pictures were a great idea.

Olivia: Each table represents a different country. The family pictures were Ana's idea. Every family in our class is included! And we have at least one kind of food from every nationality that is represented in our class.

Mr. O'Brien: Who thought of the music?

Nicholas: Cody did! He made a great playlist. We have everything from bagpipes to polka!

Mr. O'Brien: And the cookies look fantastic! How will I choose what to try?

Olivia: It looks like every person in our class brought homemade cookies. There are so many different kinds!

Mr. O'Brien: I know! I want to sample them all, but I'm afraid my clothes won't fit tomorrow!

(Cody and Ana enter from stage right.)

Cody: Guess what.

Mr. O'Brien: I have no idea! What do you guys have planned now?

Cody: Nothing! I just wanted you to know we've already made more than $1,800! There are still a ton of people waiting in line, too.

Mr. O'Brien: Wow! I guess we won't need to have another fund-raiser for the class trip.

Ana: Isn't that awesome?

Mr. O'Brien: My class is awesome!

Cody: Can I stop worrying about my social studies grade, now?

Mr. O'Brien: I think everyone deserves an A+! You really came through! Compared to what I was imagining, this is fantastic. I am so proud of all of you.

Cody: What can I say, I'm a genius! I'm also dying for some of my grandma's pizza. Let's eat, everyone!

Nicholas: Wait a minute! Did you say pizza? Pizza's not on the menu!

Cody: *(Grins.)* I know. But I asked my grandma to make one just for me!

Ana: What about us?

Cody: It's a big one. I'll share! Come on!

The End

Adapting Readers' Theater Scripts

Readers' theater can be done very simply. Performers just read their lines from scripts. They don't have to memorize them! And, they don't have to move around. The performers sit on chairs or stools while reading their parts.

Adapted Readers' Theater: This looks more like a regular play. The performers wear makeup and costumes. The stage has scenery and props. The cast moves around to show the action. Performers can still read from their scripts.

A Puppet Show: Some schools and libraries have puppet collections. Or students can create puppets. Students make the puppets be the actors. They read their scripts for their puppets.

Teaching Guides

Readers' Theater Teaching Guides are available online at **abdopublishing.com**. Each guide includes printable scripts, reading levels for each character, and additional production tips for each play. Get yours today!

Websites

To learn more about Readers' Theater, visit **booklinks.abdopublishing.com**. These links are routinely monitored and updated to provide the most current information available.